T0194933

MOSES AND THE BIG BANG

SCIENCE AND DIVINE CREATION

KEN GOSS

WESTBOW
PRESS®
A DIVISION OF THOMAS NELSON
& ZONDERVAN

Scripture taken from the King James Version of the Bible.

THE HOLY BIBLE, NEW INTERNATIONAL VERSION®, NIV® Copyright © 1973, 1978, 1984, 2011 by Biblica, Inc.® Used by permission. All rights reserved worldwide.

This book is a work of non-fiction. Unless otherwise noted, the author and the publisher make no explicit guarantees as to the accuracy of the information contained in this book and in some cases, names of people and places have been altered to protect their privacy.

WestBow Press books may be ordered through booksellers or by contacting:

WestBow Press
A Division of Thomas Nelson & Zondervan
1663 Liberty Drive
Bloomington, IN 47403
www.westbowpress.com
1 (866) 928-1240

Because of the dynamic nature of the Internet, any web addresses or links contained in this book may have changed since publication and may no longer be valid. The views expressed in this work are solely those of the author and do not necessarily reflect the views of the publisher, and the publisher hereby disclaims any responsibility for them.

Any people depicted in stock imagery provided by Thinkstock are models, and such images are being used for illustrative purposes only. Certain stock imagery © Thinkstock.

ISBN: 978-1-9736-1102-8 (sc)
ISBN: 978-1-9736-1101-1 (e)

Library of Congress Control Number: 2017919386

Print information available on the last page.

WestBow Press rev. date: 01/18/2018

CONTENTS

DEDICATION

This book is dedicated to my family, for whom it was written.

Preface

Moses and the Big Bang started as a series of essays that I planned to give to my children and grandchildren at an appropriate time to teach them about my faith and to strengthen their faith. When I realized that several of those essays dealt with responsibility to a creator God, I decided to merge those essays into a book and share it with a broader audience. The fact that the first ten words of the Bible are "In the beginning God created the heavens and the earth" tells us that the message of a creator God is foundational to all other beliefs about God. This is why the anti-God forces have attacked this concept so vigorously. This book attempts to defuse those attacks.

ACKNOWLEDGMENTS

I owe a special thanks to my sister, Sharon Duncan, without whose support this book might not have happened.

I was born into a fundamental Christian family. At the age of eight, I received Jesus Christ as my Lord and King. In my sixty-plus years, I have attended church regularly. I have studied religious subjects both independently and in some college level classes, but I am not a theologian. I have studied several languages, but I am not a linguist. I have a degree in engineering, and I have worked as an engineer for more than forty years, but I am not a scientist.

Growing up in a Christian family, I was taught early to believe in God and to accept the Bible as His Holy Word to mankind. Added to that has been my studies and my experiences, which have confirmed to me that God does exist and the Bible is His Word. However, at the same time I have studied enough science to have a fair amount of trust in many of the published observations and conclusions of the scientific community. For most of my adult life, the orthodoxy of the fundamental Christian community has insisted on their interpretations of the Bible, including the account of creation, and the scientific community has insisted on the accuracy of their interpretations of their observations. I have struggled to find the truth between these two positions. That is the subject of this book.

CHAPTER 1

HISTORY

For millennia, men and women of many faiths and belief systems have accepted that there is a creator God who is responsible for the creation of the natural world. Almost every religious belief system, from the most advanced to the most primitive, has some form of creator and some form of creation account. In the Judeo-Christian and Muslim religions, the divinely inspired account of that creation was recorded by Moses several thousand years ago and is contained in the book of Genesis, the first book in the collection of ancient documents that Christians today call the Bible.

The book of Genesis tells us that God created everything in six days and rested on the seventh. It is a straightforward account that the least educated among us can understand, but it is also deep and complex enough to hold the interest of the most inquiring and scholarly. Thus, it has been the subject of many interpretations and understandings.

Fundamentalist Christians, who favor a literal interpretation, believe God created everything in six earth days of twenty-four hours each. In 1658, Archbishop

James Ussher used the genealogies in Genesis to place the whole of creation at about six thousand years ago.

However, this is not the only interpretation made by godly scholars. You only need to search the internet for phrases like *day age creationism, gap theory of old earth creation, theistic evolution, apparent age theory, punctuated twenty-four-hour theory, scientific creationism, twenty-four-hour creation theory, framework interpretation of genesis,* or *historical creationism* to see that godly scholars for centuries or even millennia have not always agreed on the proper interpretation of the creation account in Genesis. Each of the several interpretations has strong points and weak points. I will not rehash them here, but I encourage you to look them up to get the basics of each one.

Critics of the six-day and six-thousand-years chronology find apparent gaps and discrepancies in the timeline. They prefer to interpret the Genesis account as a myth or morality story, meant to teach us that while God is the creator, the details of the story are not intended to be scientifically accurate.

As far back as Aristotle in the fourth century BC, people have had theories about the natural formation of the earth. However, the eighteenth-century man considered to be father of modern geology, with his theories of slow, gradual development of the earth over geologic ages, is James Hutton. He observed the earth around him and concluded that there was a long history recorded in the rocks. His theories regarding a long history of development of the earth were in direct contrast to much of the religious teaching of that day and to beliefs that are still held by many today.

In the late nineteenth century, Charles Darwin observed the natural world around him and wrote *On the Origin of Species*, which theorizes that the diversity we see in the world around us originated from a simple single cell and evolved through a random process of natural selection to more complex forms, ultimately producing humans. Darwin observed small variations within species and extrapolated a theory that, with enough of these small variations and with the survival of those best adapted to their environment, those small variations would evolve over long periods of time into new species.

Regardless of several weaknesses in his logic, which Darwin recognized, and regardless of Darwin's view that evolution was a method God used to create the species, his theory has been grasped by anti-God people who interpret it to mean that no God is required to create the natural world. The scientific world began to expand on Darwin's theory, adding observations that they interpreted as evidence to support it and formulating experiments to prove it. However, Darwin only addressed the development of diverse species of biological life. He did not address the creation of the physical materials needed to support life. He also did not address the origin of that first single cell. What is more, even Darwin said that a major weakness of his theory was the lack of any fossil record of transition life-forms, a fact that is still true today despite more than a hundred years of intense searching by the scientific community.

So for nearly two centuries there has been a conflict between science and religion regarding the origins of all things. This conflict has become a conflict over the existence of a creator God. On the one hand, the faithful believe God does exist, the scriptures are His inspired Word, and His Word is infallible. If the first chapter of the Bible is not totally true and accurate, every lesson in the whole collection is called into question.

On the other hand, those who want to believe that man is the ultimate intellect and authority in the universe refuse to accept that they are responsible to any higher authority— and especially not to one they cannot experience with their five senses. They see the seven days of Genesis as a foolish religious belief that has no basis in fact.

This conflict has become quite bitter at times and has spilled over into public policy. In the United States, freedom *of* religion has often been misinterpreted to mean freedom *from* religion (except atheism). As a result, public schools have been forbidden to teach that there is a God who created all things. They are compelled instead to teach that all things developed naturally by a process of evolution, which requires no God.

I grew up in such a school environment. At the same time, I attended church faithfully. I then enrolled in a Christian college in the late sixties, where some attempt was made to reconcile the two positions—but with little success. I have multiple reasons to believe there is a creator God, and I have enough doubt in the conclusions made by the scientific community about their observations to reject their belief in a godless process. Yet I am less than satisfied with the conventional attempts by the Christian community to harmonize the account of Genesis with scientific observations of the natural world.

Today, nearly fifty years after my school days, science has learned a lot more about the universe and about our biology. While my understanding of the latest discoveries is limited, I am coming to see a pattern that reconciles Genesis and science better than any of the explanations I have heard before. That is the subject of this book. Do science and scripture tell the same story?

CHAPTER 2

PHILOSOPHY

Let's begin with some basic philosophy. If there is a creator God, and if the Bible is His Word to His created creatures, there are several things we must stipulate.

First, we are taught that God is truth. He cannot lie. That rules out a popular attempt to reconcile Genesis and science that says that things look old to scientists even though the Bible seems to say they were created recently, because even though God created them recently, He created them with an old appearance. If God created everything to look old when they are, in fact, not old, then He has not been truthful. That does not square with what we know about a God of truth. In fact, saying God made things look old that are not really old is calling God a liar and probably qualifies as blasphemy.

Second, if the Bible is the infallible Word of God communicating His truth to His creation, then honest, sincere individuals who read that truth should all come to the same understanding of it. However, people read God's Word with human biases that affect their interpretation. If the words in the Bible were not interpreted differently by different people, we would not have dozens of different Christian churches and denominations. The Bible, especially Genesis, was written several thousand years ago in a language that is no longer spoken. Even though linguists have a lot of knowledge about those ancient languages, no language is ever completely stable for long periods of time. We only have to look at the English translation of the Bible that was done some four hundred years ago by a team of scholars assembled by the English king James and compare that language to the English we speak today to understand that phrases, expressions, and nuances change over time. Even today, the English language spoken in England uses different phrases and expressions than the English language spoken in most of North America. Literary and poetic techniques can be subtle and easy to miss in older languages. The account of Genesis in the Bible was written in the Hebrew language as spoken some four millennia ago, which is not necessarily the Hebrew language that is spoken today. Although words and literary style are important, it is hard to be dogmatic about a particular understanding of the subtleties of the language.

Third, the Bible tells us that creation is the handiwork of God and that it declares His glory. If there is any observed truth about God's creation, it is true because God made it true. By observing the created universe that is His handiwork, we learn something about the glory of God.

Therefore, anything we learn by observing the physical universe must be in agreement with that which a truthful God has said in His Word.

The scientific method consists of observations that lead to theories, which are then proven or disproven by testing, resulting in conclusions about the natural laws that govern our universe. This method may have its origins as early as the tenth century in Iraq, but it exploded in Europe in the late-sixteenth and early-seventeenth centuries with people (thinkers and scientists) like Galileo and Kepler. As instruments have supplemented our powers of observation, the understanding of the universe has exploded. These basic understandings of the laws of nature, which are developed and proven by pure science, have led to an explosion of knowledge that engineers have used and applied to fashion much of our modern world.

At its most basic, science is the discipline of observing the physical universe that was created by God. Observation and measurement lead to theories. When tested with experiments and proven accurate, theories lead to conclusions, which discover or define truth about the natural world that God created. If science uses observation and measurement of the creation to discover truth about that creation, then whatever is observed, measured, discovered, tested, and proven true will declare the glory of God. If there is a disagreement between the interpretations of the Word of God and the conclusions from the observations of God's creation, then either the interpretation or the conclusion is wrong. They cannot disagree. So, when learned men use the basic scientific method to observe the natural universe carefully, measure it, form theories, and test those theories, they should learn truth about God's creation. However, scientists also make their conclusions about their observations with their own biases, which can affect their conclusions.

Some people argue that there is no need to reconcile the biblical account of creation with the findings of science because God's Word is true and we don't need to change it to agree with science. While that is a pious-sounding statement, I am left to wonder if I am understanding the truth of God's Word correctly or if I am understanding an interpretation made by well-educated and sincere but nonetheless biased people. Is there no room for learning better, deeper interpretations of God's Word based on what we observe and measure in His created universe? An oft-repeated principle of Bible interpretation is: "If the first sense makes sense then seek no other sense." But some of the "first sense" of orthodox interpretations of the creation account don't make sense, so I am seeking a better sense or a better interpretation.

Fourth, history has many examples of sincere men reading the Holy Scriptures and making wrong conclusions, and it has many examples of intelligent people making scientific conclusions that have been proven wrong.

Through the centuries, godly men have interpreted the infallible Word of God in light of their own biases and perspectives and have just plain gotten it wrong. A classic example of this misinterpretation was the Jewish expectations of a Messiah, which were based on their interpretation of prophecies in the scriptures. The prophecies were true, but their interpretation was so wrong that they rejected and crucified Him when He arrived. Another classic misinterpretation was the belief that since man was the pinnacle of God's creation, the earth must be the center of the heavens or universe. We now know that to be wrong.

But the church is not the sole proprietor of erroneous conclusions. Through the centuries, scientists have made observations of nature and drawn wrong conclusions from what they have observed. They once believed that since gold and lead were both very soft and heavy, there must be a way to convert lead into gold. Alchemists tried to find that secret for centuries. Scientists also believed for many years that the development of the earth took place in a uniform environment of slow, gradual changes. We now know that the history of the earth is marked by major catastrophes and non-uniformities.

These are only a few examples of history's long list of errors in interpretation of scripture and errors in scientific conclusions based on observations. Both religious scholars and scientists have a history of drawing the wrong conclusions from what they read or observe.

Fifth, we must recognize that the story of creation is summarized it the first ten words of the Bible for one very important reason. For several thousand years, scholarly men from Moses onward have recognized that it is critically important for mankind to recognize that we were created by God. As the creator of all things, God has the moral and legal authority to run His creation in the way that pleases Him. It is His right to set the rules of both the physical world and the spiritual world. He is the ultimate authority in all things. Without a creator god who has supreme and absolute authority, there is no foundation for any system of morality.

Chapter 3

BASIC FACTS

Historians generally agree that Genesis, the first book of the Bible, was written by Moses. Genesis traces the formation of the Hebrew nation from the time of the first man until the birth of the nation. Moses himself tells us that he was a Hebrew baby who was adopted by an Egyptian princess and raised as an Egyptian prince until about the age of forty. As an Egyptian prince, he would have been educated in all the knowledge of Egypt. Since Egypt was a world power and a center of learning, we can probably safely assume that he had at his disposal all the literary, political, religious, engineering, and scientific knowledge available in the world at that time. The scientific understanding of the Egyptians would have been rudimentary by today's standards, and the scientific understandings of the common person in the nation of Israel for whom Genesis was written would have been even more limited. That is not to say that they were ignorant or less intellectually evolved than we are today. They knew enough to build chariots, irrigation works, houses, temples, and other very large structures. It is saying that the collective scientific knowledge of mankind then was less than today, and the tools required to study fine details were not yet developed. (By the way, most high school graduates today could not build a working chariot if they had to.)

As with most ancient cultures, Moses would have been familiar with the movements of the stars. However, this would have been limited to the movements he could see with the naked eye, since telescopes were not invented until thousands of years later.

As a prince of Egypt, Moses would have been literate and familiar with many languages. He probably had read almost everything available at the time and was undoubtedly familiar with many languages and literary styles. The account of Genesis in the Bible was written in the Hebrew language as spoken in Moses's day, but it might have included literary styles from other languages of that day. Linguists believe they understand the exact meaning of each word and phrase. However, languages evolve over time. Idioms may have existed that are no longer understood.

On the scientific front, in the mid-twentieth century, Einstein proved that all matter consists of energy, and matter and energy are interchangeable. He mathematically proved his famous formula, $E=MC^2$ (energy = mass times the speed of light squared). Later, his formula was physically proven when it became the basis for all atomic energy. It was a radical new concept. In conventional chemical combustion, fuel burns in oxygen and converts some molecules into other molecules releasing energy, but atoms never change. In conventional combustion, if you gathered up all of the products of the combustion and weighed them, they would have the same mass as the fuel and oxygen you started with. Conversely, atomic energy splits atoms. It converts some large atoms into other smaller atoms, releasing atomic energy. In a nuclear reaction, the end products have less mass than the nuclear fuel you started with. The difference is mass that was converted to energy. So, mass can be converted to energy, and energy can be converted to mass.

The material world we see, feel, and smell around us is built from a fairly small number of basic particles. So far, physicists have identified only 17 subatomic particles. These subatomic particles combine to make up the 118 elements (atoms) of the periodic table. Those elements, or atoms, combine to form millions of molecules, which chemists arrange and rearrange into some very amazing products that we take for granted in our twenty-first-century lives.

Physicists also tell us there are only four basic forces in the universe:

1) The strong nuclear force holds the nuclei of atoms together

2) The weak nuclear force is responsible for radioactive decay and fusion

3) Gravity causes all mass to be attracted to all mass

4) The electromagnetic force is the basis for most of what we commonly recognize as energy

Even today, with all our knowledge of the universe, physicists know there is more out there that we still do not understand. They call it dark matter. They know it is there because they see the effects of its gravity, but they cannot detect it with any of our instruments. They estimate that seventy percent of the mass of the universe is this dark matter.

In the early twentieth century, Edwin Hubble discovered that the universe is expanding. Since then, astronomers with some very powerful telescopes have observed and measured the tracks of the universe of stars, galaxies, and other heavenly bodies. They can see and measure the position, the speed, and the direction of travel of these objects. When they play the video in reverse and project the travel speed and direction backward in time, they find that all the stars, all the mass of material in the universe, converges on a point in space about fourteen billion years ago. This is what has led to the big bang theory, which says that all matter sprang into existence from a single point of energy called a singularity. The singularity was so incredibly concentrated and dense that the materials of the universe and the laws of physics as we know them today could not have existed. In fact, scientists believe that in the beginning, there was only one pure super force, which then split into the seventeen subatomic particles plus the four basic forces during a period that they call the inflation of the universe.

Still, physicists have no viable theory for the source of the incredibly concentrated and dense singularity. They don't know what caused it to start to inflate and split or the source of the pattern or design for a universe of incredible complexity built from a small handful of subatomic particles and basic forces.

Scientists have the capability to run some very sophisticated computer models using the natural laws of physics and mathematical relationships, which have been repeatedly proven by experimentation in the past few hundred years. These models are the same kinds of models that engineers use extensively to design everything from toasters to giant earthmoving machines. When scientists formulate a theory about the formation of our solar system, including the earth and all the planets and moons, they can run those theories through a computer model to see if the theory is viable or if it is nonsense. Those models confirm a timeline, which indicates that the planet we call earth, the third rock from the sun, started to form about four billion years ago.

When we observe the world around us and try to determine the origins of our little corner of the universe and the life that inhabits it, scientists use several different dating methods. These range from tree rings, ice layers in glaciers, and geological strata to rates of radioactive decay. All the dating methods are based on assumptions of one kind or another, so they are only as valid as the underlying assumptions. We also need to be careful of circular reasoning, which says that my fossil is a million years old because it was found in a layer of sediment that you say is a million years old, and you say your sediment is a million years old because it contained my fossil which I say is a million years old.

Clearly, some of the dating methods are more reliable and more precise while others are less reliable and less precise. However, taken together, the multiple dating methods suggest that planet earth came into existence a few billion years ago, and the stuff we call life came into existence a few hundred thousand years ago. However, truly human life is only known to have existed for a few thousand years.

CHAPTER 4

WHAT IS A DAY?

Much of the conflict between science and scripture centers on a timeline. For hundreds or even thousands of years, well-intentioned, godly people have read the words of Genesis with a literal, earth-centered interpretation of the word *day* or *Yom* in the original Hebrew. Each of the six work days of creation (not the seventh day) are defined by the phrase "the evening and the morning were the ___ day". The closest translation of the phrase is that it means a workday. Most of us would say that a workday is defined as a morning through to an evening, but God inspired Moses to say the reverse. I suspect there is some significance to that wording. I speculate that He is saying that the evening marked the end of one workday and the morning marked the beginning of the next workday. If so, then is He saying that He completed a creative work, then there was a pause or an interlude with no creative activity between the end of one creative work, or day, and the beginning of the next creative work, or day. During this pause, I assume that the processes He set in motion by His creative works were still running and developing the full potential of that creative work.

Also consider that a major characteristic of God it that He is eternal. He had no beginning, and He will have no end. He is timeless. This is described in many ways, but one of the more familiar descriptions is repeated in a couple passages of scripture, which say that with God a day is as a thousand years and a thousand years is as a day. Note that this is not a mathematical equation (1 day = 1000 years). It is an expression to mean that God is eternal and timeless. So, how long is the workday of an eternal God? Many of the most fundamental and orthodox theologians have dogmatically interpreted it to mean a twenty-four-hour earth day, or one rotation of the axis of planet earth, the third rock from the sun, at its current rate of rotation. These people teach that God created the world in 144 hours and then He rested for 24 hours. That seems to be a very earth-centered interpretation, much the same as early scholars believing that the earth was the center of the universe and the whole universe rotated around the earth. It also seems to be a very temporal concept of an eternal God.

If God is as unimaginably expansive as an observation of the universe would suggest, why would He define the timeline of creation in terms of one rotation of the axis of a relatively insignificant planet rotating around a relatively insignificant star in a relatively insignificant galaxy? Also, was the time interval that of a day measured several thousand years ago or that of a day measured today, since we know that the speed of the earth's rotation is slowing by a very small amount each year?

If the phrase used in Genesis means a workday, and if a workday means the daylight hours, then we also need to recognize that all workdays are not the same duration. On most of the earth surface, the length of a sunrise to sunset workday changes with the seasons. In some places, it changes dramatically. So, are the six workdays of Genesis all the same length?

While I have no doubt that God could have created everything from nothing in 144 hours, or even in 144 seconds, I wonder if He really did choose to complete His work in that amount of time. I think we have to separate the creative works from the developmental works. A creative work would be when He made something from nothing. He created something that had never before existed. A development work would be when He used the laws and processes that He had earlier created to develop the full potential of that creation.

I believe most of the miracles recorded in scripture occurred when God used the existing laws of nature, laws He created at the time of creation, in ways that we have never seen and are unable to duplicate in order to accomplish His purposes. Today God is resting from His creative works, but He is active in His developmental work.

When Jesus turned water into wine, was it a creative work or an application of the laws of nature that we do not yet understand? When Moses parted the sea, was it a creative work or an application of the laws of nature? Today, engineers are applying the laws of nature in ways that would have seemed miraculous to people only a few decades ago. We call it *creating* a new product, but it is really *developing* a new product. I expect God's created works were most likely instantaneous, while the development of the full potential of that created work may have taken some longer period of time.

If we accept that the term "the evening and the morning was the _____ day" is a poetic or idiomatic expression that can mean simply that each day is a phase of creation or each day is a specific creative work, the timeline of Genesis can easily agree with what we observe as a timeline in the creation that declares the glory of God. In fact, doesn't a 14 billion-year timeline declare the glory of an eternal timeless God just as well as or maybe better than a 7-day, 168-hour timeline?

On the extreme end of the time spectrum, physicists talk of a unit of time measurement called Planck time. One Planck time unit is ten to the minus forty-three seconds. That means a decimal point with forty-three zeros behind it and then a one. There are more Planck time units in one second than there have been seconds in fourteen billion years. Scientists theorize that much of the big bang, or the inflation of the singularity, happened in a few thousand units of Planck time, or just a small fraction of a second. For practical purposes, that means instantaneously. So, while some of the divine workdays of Genesis might have been billions of years long, some of them might have been almost infinitesimally short. Again, if God is timeless, the length of a workday can be whatever He wants it to be.

A small number of physicists today have started to contemplate the existence of time and what it means to physics. Is it constant and fixed or is it flexible? Has it always been the same as it is today? Science orthodoxy today assumes that time is constant and that it has always been constant, exactly the same as it is today. However, there are physicists who are looking at time in a deeper way and questioning the orthodox view of time. Did the creation of the universe include the creation of time?

One more thought about the day. If the day is a twenty-four-hour earth day, and if God rested on the seventh day, what did He do on the eighth day? On the other hand, if the day is a creative workday, with a time length that relates to an eternal God, the seventh day could also be much longer than twenty-four hours. Today we don't see any new laws of physics changing our environment, and we don't see any new species of plants or animals or other life-forms being created. So, can we say that while today God is very active in His development and management efforts, He is resting from His creative efforts? If today He is resting from His creative works, are we living in the seventh day? More on that later.

On a different note, I believe when God inspired Moses to write the account of creation, He was considering His audience. If God had inspired Moses to write a deeply detailed scientific account of creation, the people of Moses's day and even the majority of the population today would have been completely lost. They would have no idea what he was attempting to communicate. It seems much more likely that God inspired Moses to write an account in poetic or metaphorical language that people could understand but which could also be completely accurate when understood by those with a much greater depth of scientific knowledge which He knew He would reveal to mankind at a future time.

A creative "day" could be understood by the youngest or least educated among us. If Moses had said seven billion years or seven Planck time units instead of seven days, it might have been pretty difficult for most people to grasp. Even today people have difficulty understanding these extreme units of time. I think Moses was probably more interested in communicating that God was responsible for creation than in communicating all the complex details of how and when. The purpose of the story is to tell us that God is the creator and, as such, He has the moral and legal authority to set the rules for the behavior of His created beings and to deal with them as He sees fit.

CHAPTER 5

DAY ONE: IN THE BEGINNING

The Genesis account of creation starts with day one, or the first creative act, the creation of physical matter and light.

Science once believed the universe was eternal with no beginning and no end. We now know there was a beginning. Physicists tell us that, in the beginning, there was a singular ball of incredibly dense energy that came from somewhere. Then suddenly, for some reason, it started to inflate in what has become known as the big bang. As this ball of pure, raw energy inflated, it started to split off the four basic forces and spin off subatomic particles.

While scientists today understand that these subatomic particles are really tiny packets of energy, they do not know how to make a particle from energy. They have some rather large and sophisticated machinery that they have used to discover some of these particles by blasting them out of atoms, but they have never taken any form of energy and created even one subatomic particle. So, not only do scientists not know where the singularity came from, they don't know how or why it started to convert into physical mass and form the physical universe as we know it.

After the pure super force created a huge cloud with masses of physical particles at the subatomic level, scientists theorize that the strong nuclear force split off from that original energy ball of pure, raw force. The strong nuclear force is what holds groups of protons together in the nucleus of an atom. Since protons are all positively charged particles, they want to repel one another, but the strong nuclear force holds them together. Without the strong nuclear force, there could be no atoms and there would never be any solid matter.

Next, it seems most likely that the electromagnetic force split off from the original force. What is important here is that the electromagnetic force is what holds negatively charged electrons in orbits around positively charged nuclei. Without the electromagnetic force, there would only be a cloud or soup of atomic nuclei. There would be no atoms—nothing solid. These three things—particles from energy, strong nuclear force, and electromagnetic force—all seem to have happened in a very short time, maybe even a few Planck time units. They were created in an instant, but developed or inflated into a universe over a much longer period of time.

Scripture says that God created everything from nothing. He created the seen from the unseen. One interpretation could be that He created physical material from energy. Genesis says that in the beginning God created the heavens and the earth (the material universe) and that the earth (physical material) was without form and void, and that darkness covered the face of the deep. God is the source of the ball of energy. God is the intellect that made it convert into particles of physical matter. God is also the intellect that conceived the strong nuclear force and the electromagnetic force and made them split from the pure energy of what science calls the singularity.

The Genesis description of "without form and void" sounds like a poetic description of the formless, shapeless, vaporous cloud, or fog, of tiny subatomic particles, or atoms, that science theorizes to have existed just after the big bang. The collected mass of new physical particles was not round, oval, square, or triangular; it was without form. The new mass of physical particles was not solid or liquid; it was vaporous or void. I imagine it was something like the beautiful but slightly eerie clouds of gasses we see though our telescopes today. The phrase "darkness covered the deep" sounds obvious since light did not yet exist. The scientific theories and the Genesis account agree.

Next, scripture says that God commanded light to exist, and it came into being. Most of us today read that and have a mental image of flipping on a light switch so we can see our way around without bumping into things. However, light is much more complex than that. Science today recognizes that light is a component of the electromagnetic force, one of the four basic forces in the universe. Light is electromagnetic radiation.

The light we see is one small fraction of the total spectrum of electromagnetic radiation. Beyond the rainbow spectrum of light wavelengths that we see as colors, most of us are familiar with the terms *ultraviolet light*, which we know exists beyond one end of the spectrum, and *infrared light*, which exists beyond the other end of the spectrum. However, we are not capable of seeing either of these without instruments. Light also includes a lot of other things that we cannot see without instruments. X-rays, microwaves, radio waves, gamma rays, and much more are all technically light. Today, even magnetism and magnetic forces, including electricity, are recognized by physicists to be a form of light. It is also true that light (the electromagnetic force) is what holds atoms together. The strong nuclear force holds the nucleus of the atom together, and the electromagnetic force (light) keeps electrons attracted to and orbiting around the nucleus so they don't fly off randomly into space.

Scientists tell us that light is photon particles moving in waves. I have trouble understanding that, but I visualize it as a universe full of photons like an ocean full of water with energy traveling through that medium like waves in the ocean. That might not be totally correct physics, but it helps me to understand light. Scientists even say that magnetic attraction/repulsion is streams of photons pulling magnets together or pushing them apart. When God created light, He created all of this. Moses might have said that on day one, God created photons, or electromagnetic force. Would anyone have understood him? Moses said light. We all understand light on some level, but it leaves room for deeper scientific investigation. It is poetic, yet technically correct. Light was created in an instant, but developed into a universe of material and energy over a period of time.

Without light or electromagnetic force, there would be nothing solid in the universe and it would have remained a shapeless vaporous cloud of subatomic particles. Note that scripture says nothing about anything solid until after God created light. So, science and scripture agree that one of the earliest events in the creation of the universe was the creation of light or electromagnetic force. Science has not yet figured out why the four basic forces split off from the original single unified ball of pure, raw energy, and maybe not the exact sequence, but scripture tells us that God spoke and it happened. When God said, "Let there be light," I expect He made the light, or electromagnetic force, split off from the original pure super force/ball of energy.

Note too that without light there would be no means to transmit energy and information from one physical body to another physical body across the expanse of space. So, light has become a metaphor for God dealing with His created creatures. People who are walking in light are walking in communication with God and receive energy/power from God.

Now, please pause and reflect for a moment on the unimaginable immensity of a God who can supply the energy to make the whole universe. If a few grams of mass are converted to energy in a nuclear explosion that can wipe out a whole city, how powerful must a God be who can provide the energy to create all the mass of billions of billions of galaxies and stars and planets? How powerful is your God?

CHAPTER 6

DAY TWO: GRAVITY

Scientists say that during the inflation period of the universe, just after the big bang, there could not have been any gravity because all the mass would have resisted inflation. If there had been gravity, it would have pulled the mass back together and held it in a single huge ball of incredible density. Gravity had to split off from the original pure super force/ball of energy sometime after the big bang, after the inflation was well under way. Again, maybe it was a few seconds or a few Planck time units, and maybe it was millions of years.

We think of gravity as the force that holds our feet on the ground and makes our bathroom scales wind up to higher numbers than we like. We also think of gravity as the force that makes the moon orbit the earth and pull on the oceans to make tides. It makes the earth and planets orbit the sun, and it makes the solar system orbit within the Milky Way galaxy. Gravity does that and much more. Gravity is also the force that pulled together loose simple atoms out of a shapeless cloud of materials into larger and larger clumps of atoms until those clumps became planets and stars and galaxies and all sorts of heavenly bodies.

Science says that the first atoms to form out of the cloud of subatomic particles were only the small atoms like hydrogen and helium. Those small atoms were pulled together into massive stars by gravity. With the intense gravity in those huge stars, those simple atoms were pulled into dense, hot concentrations where they underwent fusion reactions to produce progressively larger and heavier atoms, which make up the heavier elements we have today. This fusion reaction is what powers our own sun. Science says that without gravity, the whole universe would consist of only the smallest simplest atoms like hydrogen (no oxygen, no carbon, no gold, and so on) and the shapeless cloud of particles would have stayed shapeless and vaporous and never developed into anything. Gravity makes the universe what it is today. Hence, it merits its own special day in the creation narrative.

Scripture says that on day two, or the second creative act, God separated the waters above from the waters below. When I read that, I ask myself what is so significant about making clouds that it merits a special day of creation, a special place in the narrative. Then I realize that the thing you need in order to make light water vapor stay up and heavier liquid water stay down is the force of gravity, one of the four basic forces in the universe. The second great work of creation described by Moses was not clouds, but gravity. It fits the timeline scientists theorize, and it fits the timeline of the story of creation in Genesis.

Note that some scientists theorize that after particles appeared and after the strong nuclear force appeared, the next force to appear was gravity, and after gravity, light. However, God's timeline clearly says that light came before gravity. I suspect the scientific community will unanimously come to the same conclusion once they catch up to Genesis.

The concept of gravity was discovered by Isaac newton in the seventeenth century. So, while the concept of gravity and the huge implications it has on our universe would not be discovered for several millennia, God inspired Moses to write a description of gravity that could be understood by a child and still be technically accurate as a clue to our most advanced minds investigating the history and origins of the universe. Thousands of years before men recognized the existence of gravity and before physicists recognized that it could not have existed in the earliest phase of the birth of our universe, God inspired Moses not only to describe it accurately by describing one of its very visible effects, but also to put it in the right sequence of events. Once again, science and Genesis agree.

If gravity can keep the moon circling the planet earth and keep earth orbiting a star called the sun and the sun orbiting the center of a Milky Way galaxy, and if it can repeat that scene trillions of times from one end of the universe to the other, how immense must be the God who created that force? Once again, how big is your God?

CHAPTER 7

DAY THREE: DRY LAND

Scripture says that on day three, or the third creative act, God made dry land appear and separated the seas from the dry land. What kind of creative act would be required to do this? He had already created the material universe on day one, and He created gravity on day two to make the water vapor rise above the waters and to pull stars together to form the heavier elements. So, what did he need to create now to make dry land rise above the surface of the waters?

Science says that if all we had was the force of gravity, the ball of material that we call earth would be stratified with the heavier and denser materials (rocks) at the bottom or the center, the less dense materials like water covering all of the surface, and the least dense materials like gasses on top. So, what makes heavy, dense rocks rise above the surface of the water? Science tells us that the core of the earth is molten iron and rocks, so a mantle of frozen, or solid, rock floats on top of the molten center. The molten material in the center circulates with the rotation of the earth and causes the tectonic plates of solid crust to collide and rise up above the waters. It also causes volcanic activity, which raises earth above the waters. So, if the molten center of the earth is responsible for making dry land appear, what is it that keeps the center of the earth molten so all of this can happen?

I understand that the pressure of gravity alone is not sufficient to keep it molten. Other rocky planets have gravity but don't have molten cores. There needs to be another source of heat. One of the less known sources of the heat at the center of the earth is the radioactive decay of the dense materials in the core. What causes radioactive decay? Physicists tell us that the weak nuclear force, or the fourth of the basic forces in the universe, is responsible for radioactive decay. I must confess that I don't understand all of the implications of the weak nuclear force, how it operates, and what all of the effects might be, but I understand that it is responsible for radioactive decay of large, heavy atoms like uranium, plutonium, and others at the large end of the periodic table of elements. It is also responsible for the radioactive decay of isotopes of some of the less dense elements like the iron at the core of the earth.

Today one of the problems with nuclear reactors as a source of electricity is the disposal of the spent nuclear fuel. This fuel is not powerful enough to support a nuclear reaction in the core of a reactor, but it is still undergoing radioactive decay. It is still radioactive, and that makes it stay hot. The radioactive decay has a long half-life, so it will remain hot and radioactive, possibly for hundreds or thousands of years. That is what makes it so difficult and expensive to dispose of safely. The heat from that same kind of radioactive decay is part of what keeps the core of the earth molten.

When God made dry land appear above the waters on day three, He created the fourth of the basic forces that physicists recognize today. However, as with gravity and electromagnetic force, if God had inspired Moses to write that God created the weak nuclear force, most readers even today would have yawned and tuned out. So, He had Moses describe it in terms that anyone could understand, yet terms that the most educated and intelligent among us could use to gain a clue to the origins of things.

The weak nuclear force is a strange force. Not only does it limit the size of atoms by causing radioactive decay, it is also instrumental in facilitating the fusion reactions in the sun and stars where smaller atoms are fused into larger atoms. The fusion builds up larger atoms from smaller ones, but the radioactive decay prevents them from becoming too large. The heaviest of the 118 elements that we are aware of today are pretty unstable and decay pretty quickly when they are formed. If there were no weak nuclear force to decay these larger atoms, we might have lots of heavier atoms in our universe. On the other hand, if the fusion engine of the stars could not ignite without the weak nuclear force, we might never have anything larger or heavier that hydrogen. God created the balance.

The Bible doesn't seem to say it directly, but the weak nuclear force created on day three that keeps the core of the earth molten has one other effect. The circulation of the molten core of the earth is responsible for creating a magnetic field around the earth. We think of it as the force that makes a compass point to the north, but it is also the shield that keeps harmful solar radiation in the solar wind from stripping away our atmosphere and killing everything. We see this effect in the aurora borealis, or the northern lights, where charged particles from our sun slam into the magnetic shield, creating a beautiful display of lights. Mars and Venus do not have this protective shield, so their atmosphere has been blow away by the solar wind, and life cannot exist on these planets. This magnetic shield would be required to support the next acts of creation and allow life to survive.

CHAPTER 8

DAY THREE: PLANTS

Scripture says that on day three, God also created plant life. Until now, God has only created inanimate materials and forces. Now He creates something that has the capability to absorb nutrients and energy and grow into a form that is totally different from any of its components. It has the capability to reproduce itself and make more of its own kind. In short, it is alive.

The big bang theory deals with the origins of the inert and lifeless materials and the forces of the universe. It does not deal with the origins of life. The concept of evolution deals with the development of diversity of life after it was created. However, neither evolution nor the big bang deal with how life started.

The proponents of evolution theorize that life somehow spontaneously generated from inert elements energized by some mysterious coincidence or spark. If that is true, scientists should be able to create life if they can find the right combination of chemicals in the right arrangement of structure and the right amount of energy applied at just the right time. Scientists have been trying to accomplish this creation of life for more than a hundred years and have yet to accomplish anything more than to make some of the chemicals that are necessary for life.

The concept of evolution also theorizes that the diversity of life we see in the world today would have required millions of years of iterations of life-forms. However, the geologic record shows plant life for much too short a time for that to have been possible. If you do some math and statistics with the number of current and extinct plant species and the number of years scientists believe plants have been on the earth, there just aren't enough years for a random process to have made all those mutations.

Where scripture and science agree is on the sequence of life-forms being created. Both science and scripture agree that plant life appeared on our planet before any form of animal life. Science tells us that the early plant life actually generated the oxygen in our atmosphere that was necessary to support animal life. Early plant life is also responsible for the coal and oil and natural gas deposits that provide our energy today. So, it appears that God had a plan when He created plant life.

Today, we can analyze a plant and break it down into the base chemicals, but we have never created anything that can grow and reproduce. The only way we can make a living plant is to grow it from a seed or cutting from another plant. We can cross-pollinate plants to make stronger or more productive plants. We can genetically alter plants to make them resistant to pests or to make them taste better or to make them produce more, but we have never produced a new plant species. We can take a live seed that can germinate and grow into a plant, and we can make it dead so that it can no longer germinate, but we cannot take a dead seed and restore it to life. We cannot see or photograph or x-ray the life. We cannot measure the life. We cannot weigh the life. We can hold a living seed in our hands, but we cannot hold the life. We can see the symptoms of a living plant versus a dead plant, but we cannot identify the life itself. It is still a mystery to us.

There is a line of thinking that says that the days of Genesis must have been very short because plants were created before the sun was created to energize them. If the sun had not appeared within twenty-four hours, all the plants would have died. However, these same people have no problem believing that in an eternal city, a New Jerusalem, the tree of life will flourish and bear its fruits in their twelve seasons, but there will be no need of the sun. We also know that, even today, there are forms of algae that grow deep in the oceans where there is no sunshine to energize them. The lesson is that there are alternative sources of energy for plants to grow. Sunshine is certainly the primary source of energy in our world today, but has it always been this way? Is it also possible that the first plants God created did not need sunlight as we know it today in order to grow and reproduce after their kind? Is it possible that there was some other source of energy in the distant past?

Another line of thinking says that the days of creation must have been very short because insects are needed to pollinate the plant flowers so plants can reproduce, and these insects were not created until after the plants were created. Had these two creative events been more than a few hours apart, all of the plants would have failed to reproduce. The problem with this line of thinking is that it does not allow for alternative methods of pollination. I have seen tomatoes raised in screened-in greenhouses where there are no insects. The operators of these facilities go around daily and pollinate the blossoms by touching them with a vibrating tuning fork. So, there are alternate methods to pollinate plants. Is it possible that alternative pollination mechanisms have existed in the past?

Many have interpreted the words of Genesis to mean that God spoke and instantly the earth was covered with thick, lush, mature vegetation. While God is certainly capable of such a scenario, and He certainly could have done it that way, is that the only way He could have done it? The operative question becomes: Did He really do it that way? Does the evidence that we see in

Ken Goss

God's creation tell us that He made all mature plants in a matter of hours a few thousand years ago? Or does the evidence tell us that God created plant life and then developed the abundance and diversity that we see today by manipulating and managing a process over a period of thousands of years? The scripture never specifically says if God individually created mature plants in all of their diversity or if He created a simple microscopic alga and then directed a process of diversification that developed it into giant redwoods and everything in between. It doesn't say if the process of diversification took Planck time units or millions of years. However, when He finished the diversification, the plants reproduced according to their kinds, and since He finished the third creative act and called it good, or complete, plants have continued to reproduce according to their kinds.

It is also interesting to note that the scriptures never directly say that God created plant life on planet earth and only on planet earth. In Genesis 2 it says that God planted a Garden in Eden. If He had instantaneously covered the whole earth with mature vegetation as some propose, why would it have been necessary to plant a garden? It also says that before any shrub of the field had appeared on the earth, God created man from the dust of the earth. But we know from Genesis chapter one that man was created three days after plants were created. Now then, this is highly speculative, but is it possible that God created plant life on another planet in another solar system in another galaxy and then transported it to our planet at just the right time for it to thrive in an earthly garden? There is a line of thinking, possibly with some tantalizing evidences, that says our ancestors might have come to earth from another world or at least were influenced by alien visitors (angels?). One of many things the ancient alien theorists cite as evidence is a passage in Genesis 6. Today, astronomers are discovering that there are a lot of planets in the universe that could possibly support life. I also wonder what Jesus meant when He said, "In my father's house there are many mansions"? Did He mean a literal house, or was He referring to a universe full of habitable planets? This is very unconventional thinking, but it is intriguing.

Wherever, whenever, and however it was done, the bottom line is that God created plant life, and God developed the diversity of plant life we see today. Plants reproduce according to their kinds, and no new species are being developed because that creation is complete and God has called it good. Consider for a moment the love of a God who created plants to provide oxygen, energy, food, building and clothing materials, and beauty for the people He knew He would create later. How loving is your God?

CHAPTER 9

DAY FOUR: TIME

A superficial reading of day four, or the fourth creative act in Genesis, leads many to conclude that on day four God created the sun, the moon, and all of the heavenly bodies. This requires an earth-centered view of the universe where the earth was created first and then everything around the earth came later. This is the same view that was debunked by the observations of Galileo and Copernicus and the early astronomers and physicists. So, we conclude that while the words of the scriptures are true, our understanding of the meaning might be flawed. We know today that the universe does not orbit around the earth. If you look deeper into the account of scripture, it says that God made (or caused) the greater light to" rule" (for the purpose of regulating) the day and the lesser light to rule the night and the other heavenly bodies to determine times and seasons. I think it is saying is that on day four God created a system for measuring time. I don't think He actually created the heavenly bodies on day four, but he set them into orbits that are predictable and repeatable so that we could measure the passage of time.

We know today that the gravity God created on day two would have drawn materials together to form earth and all the heavenly bodies, and the weak nuclear force that he created on day three would have ignited the fusion reactions that power those bodies. So, what could He have created on day four to set the universal clock and calendar?

Physicists today know from analyzing the motions of the stars that there exists a form of mass that has gravity and affects the motions of those stars but is otherwise totally undetectable by our instruments. They call it dark matter. They don't know what it is, but they know something exists because they see the effect its gravity has on the orbits of the heavenly bodies in the universe. The dark matter is a bit like the wind which you cannot see. You know it exists because you can see the effects that it has on trees and flags and such. Scientists calculate that this dark matter makes up about 70 percent of the mass in the universe, and it controls the movements of the stars and galaxies, but they don't know what it is. I don't know for sure what God created at this point, but I suspect this is the point where God created the stuff physicists call dark matter and placed it where it would stabilize and control the movements of the heavenly bodies, but not interfere with the transmission of light.

Another possibility might be that He created time (the fourth dimension) as we know it at this point in the progression of His creative works. I expect that as we observe His creation in more depth, we may discover something that makes the time question clearer. Some physicists have started to ponder the existence of time and what it means to physics. Is it constant and fixed, or is it flexible? Has it always been the same as it is today? Science orthodoxy today assumes that time is constant and that it has always been constant, exactly the same as it is today. However, there are physicists who are looking at time in a deeper way and questioning the orthodox view of time.

Physicists today believe the speed of light is a hard upper limit to speed (time). They also believe that the big bang happened almost instantaneously. They talk about things happening much faster than the speed of light during those first few moments of the inflation of the universe. They talk about Planck time, which is infinitesimally small for practical purposes. Some believe the beginning events that created the seventeen subatomic particles and the four basic forces all happened in a matter of a few thousand units of Planck time or almost instantaneously. If the first moments of the existence of the universe were measured in Planck time, and today we measure time in much larger units, is it not reasonable to believe that at some point time itself might have changed? Or maybe time as we know it did not exist until day four? I expect that at some point science will catch up to scripture on the question of defining time.

Whatever the deep meaning is, I think it is clear that day four was not the creation of the heavenly bodies themselves, but rather the creation of a heavenly clock and calendar—something that an eternal God does not need, but something that His creation could not do without.

It is also important to note that when Moses wrote the book of Genesis, many cultures worshiped the sun and the moon. Moses was undoubtedly very interested in communicating that the sun and moon were created and set in their courses by a higher power, a supreme being to whom we owe all our worship. The heavenly bodies themselves are not worthy of worship, but the God who created them and set them in synchronized motions is worthy of all worship. Moses might also have been making the point that God is in control of time.

One more thought: If God created time and fixed the stars in place to give us a means to determine times and seasons, is it not reasonable to believe that when we observe the stars and measure their movements, we should trust the timeline they are telling us? If we track the paths of the stars and see that they converge at a point some fourteen billion years ago, is it not reasonable to believe that Genesis 1:1 happened about fourteen billion years ago? What is more, doesn't a fourteen-billion-year timeline declare the glory of an infinite eternal God in a very striking way? How eternal is your God?

CHAPTER 10

DAY FIVE: SEA AND AIR CREATURES

Science says that animal life began in the oceans. Depending on their particular area of study, scientists use several dating methods. Some are based on fossil records, some on geological strata, some on radioactive decay rates of rocks where fossils are found, some on radiocarbon dating, and more. Each of the methods has limitations, but together they seem to tell a fairly consistent story about the age of earth and the beginning of animal life that inhabits earth. Whatever the timeline, the basic agreement is that both scripture and science say that animal life began in the oceans. Furthermore, it began after all the basic materials and laws of physics were complete and after plant life was established.

Both scripture and science agree that before life began, all the materials and all the basic forces in the universe were in place. The proponents of unguided, random, godless evolution do not seem to deal with the first days of creation and how all of the materials and forces got here in the first place. They seem to assume that the physical materials of the universe have always been here, that time has always been the same, and that the only thing needed for life to emerge was for a fantastic series of accidents to happen. Then after life emerged, it randomly evolved through another unbelievably random string of accidents. I have studied enough statistics and probability to know that if an event requires a near infinite number of events each with a nearly infinitesimally small probability for it to happen, it takes a lot of faith to believe it happened without intelligent intervention. Quite honestly, I think it takes more faith to believe that everything happened with no God than it does to believe that an omnipotent, omniscient, eternal God created everything.

Genesis says that on day five, or the fifth creative act, God created the water life and birds. So, what is unique about sea life and birds that groups them together and sets them apart from land life, which is created later? Many folks have asked which creatures are sea creatures and which are land creatures. In which group do the amphibians belong? Also, in which group are the insects? It seems to me that the one thing the creatures created on day five have in common is that they reproduce by laying eggs and hatching them. I suspect Moses is saying that God created all the creatures that lay eggs and hatch their young at this point. That would include fish, reptiles, insects, birds, and so on. Whatever it is, for the first time in the progression of creation, God has now created creatures that can not only absorb nutrients and grow and reproduce, but are mobile and can react to their environment. They can move in search of their food instead of being rooted in one place. They are programed with instincts that define and control their behavior. They have senses of sight, touch, smell, hearing, and taste. They have nervous systems and brains to process these senses.

So what exactly did God create? In a word, He created life. He used the physical materials of the universe to fashion bodies that would support the life, but the thing that was created was the life itself. Just as with plants, we can recognize when a batch of cells has life and when it has no life. We can dissect a body and identify each of the parts in excruciating detail. We can examine the DNA and see the distinctness not only of each species, but of individuals within that species. We can watch the working of the brain on scanners of various kinds. However, we cannot see, touch, smell, hear, taste, or measure in any way the life itself. We cannot create life from a batch of inanimate materials. God created the life, and He created the means, in fact the only means, for that life to reproduce and make more life. We can use the process He created to produce more life, but we cannot produce life aside from that natural process.

Scripture does not say if God created fully mature adults or if he created eggs that needed to hatch. It does not say if they were all created in an instant or if the diversity developed over a longer period of time. It also does not say if each kind was created individually or if a single life was created and then a process of diversification managed by God led to the diversity we see today. Genesis does say that He blessed the creatures He had created and told them to be fruitful and increase in number to fill the seas and the air, so I might understand that to mean that He probably created one mating pair of each species and then allowed them to multiply and fill the earth through the process He had created.

Some evidence in the geologic record seems to indicate there was a progression in complexity through a period of time. Genesis does not give us that level of detail. However, if the day of genesis is truly a divine workday, it seems reasonable to assume there was probably a progression to the work. So, could God have started day five by creating the thing we call life and then continued and finished the day by managing a process of developing the diversification of species? Even science seems to agree that there have been times in the history of our planet when new species were appearing very frequently, and other times when the diversity was pretty stable. Whatever the process was and whatever the timeline, there came a point when God had completed the creation of all the kinds of fish and fowl and called it good, or complete. From that point onward, those life-forms reproduced after their own kinds and no new egg-laying species have been developed or created (or evolved). That work is complete.

Note that science and scripture seem to agree that there was a tremendous diversity of egg-laying creatures on earth before any land creatures arrived. It takes only a casual observer to recognize that in our world today we see many species of egg laying creatures. However, even with the diversity that we see today, we are only seeing a portion of the total that was created. Many species have become extinct. On the other hand, we are not aware of any new species that have recently evolved or been created. That work is complete.

Just as with plants, scientists have figured out how to manipulate genetics with crossbreeding and DNA modifications. We can tell you every chemical that is in the makeup of a body. We can heal diseases, and we can treat some pretty serious wounds. We can perform surgeries to correct defects in major organs. We can do in-vitro fertilization. We can artificially inseminate. We can even resuscitate animals that are in comas or near death. However, not only have we never created a life, we have never developed or evolved a new species from an existing species. What is more, in those cases where there is a random natural genetic mutation, it always results in a creature that is weaker and less adaptable to the environment, not stronger and better able to adapt and compete. The observations of science support Genesis. The creation of the egg-laying species is complete.

Consider for a moment the intellect of a God who can conceive of an animal body. The eye alone is a marvelous structure, but multiply that by brains and ears and all the various systems that make up most animal bodies, and you get a creator god with some pretty awesome intelligence. Then add in the mystery stuff that we call life, and you get an unimaginable intelligence. How smart is your God?

CHAPTER 11

DAY SIX: LAND CREATURES

Genesis says that on day six, or the sixth creative act, God created all land animal life. I am assuming this means everything from the tiniest to the most gigantic of creatures, everything currently living and everything that has become extinct. The definition of land creatures includes every creature that carries their young internally and gives birth, as opposed to egg-laying creatures. I am left wondering why two days or two creative acts? Why separate the land creatures from the sea and air creatures? Why these required two creative works is something I don't understand. Is there a difference in the DNA structures or some other fundamental difference? Or do creatures that give birth have a different spirit or a different *life*, something different we are not capable to detect and measure? Is there some fundamental difference that science has observed beyond hatching versus birthing? Is the essence of life different for birthing creatures and hatching creatures?

As with the sea life, we don't know if birthing animals were created as fully developed adults or if they were created immature and had to grow up. We don't know if God made a mud statue of each animal and then made it come alive, or if He made each higher species to be born from a mother of a lower species. We also don't know if God chose to create each species individually in a nanosecond, or if He chose to develop them progressively over a workday thousands of years long. We don't know if He created all species simultaneously in an instant or if He used a process of diversification, building more complex or refined animals from simpler species over a period of time.

Am I signing up to the theistic evolution concept? If, by theistic evolution, you mean that God started the process and then allowed random mutations and survival of the fittest to create the diversity we see today, then no, I am not signing up for that. I do not believe there was anything random about it. If, by theistic evolution, you mean that God used a process of developing one species from another, directing each change and leaving nothing to chance, then maybe I am open to that possibility. Whether God created each species separately and individually or whether He used existing species to hatch or give birth to new species, He directed each step of the process. Whether God created all the species in an instant, in twenty-four hours, or over a period of thousands of years, He controlled the timeline.

This might also be a good point to note that while many of us have a real problem with random evolution of the separate species, we all accept evolution within a species. In other words, did God create a Cocker Spaniel and a Beagle and a Great Dane, or did He create a dog that He then developed into wolves and coyotes and foxes and dogs as we know them today? If we did not have evolution within a species, we might all be stuck with wolves or tigers for house pets. Today, most of the breeds we have, from corn and wheat to cows and chickens, are a result of crossbreeding and developing new variations within the species. People have developed a lot of new breeds within a species, but we have never developed a new species, though some have tried. People have tried to crossbreed animals between species with no success. It seems that today the species are fixed. When God saw that it was good, He was saying that the diversification was complete and no more cross-species diversification was necessary or possible.

As I have said about plant life, we can dissect an animal and learn all about the circulatory system and the nervous system and the bones and the muscles and everything else. We can analyze the chemicals in each part of the animal, and we can identify individual animals by their unique DNA. We can understand the behavior and psychology of an animal. We can tell when an animal is alive or dead, and we can certainly make a living animal dead. We can even bring animals back from the brink of death. However, we cannot identify the life itself. We cannot put life under a microscope and examine it. We have never been able to take a set of inert, lifeless chemicals and make them come alive. It takes God to do that.

Consider for a bit the stability created by a DNA system the only allows like kinds to reproduce. If this were not true, we might have creatures that are part elephant and part giraffe or part dog and part alligator, or any other surreal combination. So, how constant and unchangeable is your God?

CHAPTER 12

DAY SIX: MAN

Evolutionary theory says that humans evolved from a subhuman species commonly referred to as apes or monkeys. Evolutionists point to a lot of examples of skeletons with similarities (but still a lot of differences) and even to DNA similarities between humans and some subhuman species. They show pictures of a chain of progressively more complex and capable creatures that they say proves their concept, but they often fail to say that these are artists' renderings based on very limited skeletal remains. In point of fact, there are no fossils of true definitive transitional species. The transitions are largely in the imagination of scientists. That imagination might be backed by a solid knowledge of anthropology and skeletal features, but it is still largely imagination, speculation, and theory.

Nonetheless, science does seem to have some solid evidence from the geologic fossil record that indicates that humans are the last species to have appeared on planet Earth. We also know that the recorded human history starts pretty recently in geologic terms. We only have a few thousand years of recorded human history, and maybe a few thousand more of evidence, which indicates some level of human capabilities. We also have evidence that there have been several early civilizations of near-human creatures or proto humans that are now extinct. We can study the evidences that these proto humans left behind, and we can learn a lot about them. We can see their physical features, and we can look at their tools. We can study the structures they left behind and learn about their lifestyle. However, we can only speculate and theorize about their emotions, conscience, and spirit. We cannot determine if they were truly human or simply a near-human creature.

Evolutionary science says that humans are the pinnacle of the evolutionary process. Starting with a single-cell life-form, evolution resulted when small, natural changes or mutations developed progressively higher life forms until humans were the result. If this is true science, then it would be based on an observation that has been proven to be true. If man has evolved into what we are today, and if we will continue to evolve into something better, then we should be able to see a pattern of that progression. We should be seeing super humans evolving in our culture today and not just in comic books.

While there may be a pattern of higher technical achievements, especially in recent history, I do not see a pattern of improvement today in the human character or the human physical body. There is clear evidence for a progression in the knowledge and capabilities of humankind, but this simply means that humans are capable of learning from previous generations and passing along the technical knowledge. However, people are still violent, greedy, selfish, lazy, and uncivil. Our jails are still full. We still have wars. We still have murders. We still have theft. We still have addictions. The list is long. We still have health problems, and we still die at about seventy or eighty years of age. An unbiased observation of human history does not support the concept of an evolving and progressively more refined or a more capable human being.

The creation account in Genesis relates that after creating everything else, God said, "Let Us make man in Our image," and then made a man from the dust of the earth and breathed into him the breath of life. The chronology of begats and begottens in Genesis tells us that the first humans appeared only a few thousand years ago.

The timing of the Genesis account and the evidence that science has found are very similar. Both say that man is the ultimate and last species to appear on earth, and both say that the earliest true humans only appeared a few thousand years ago. So, at this level, science and Genesis agree.

The conventional mental picture of man's creation is one of an Almighty God playing in the mud to make a statue of a man and then doing mouth-to-mouth to make him come alive. Somehow, I suspect this language is mostly a poetic way of saying that God made a man with a physical body consisting of the elements of the universe. Presumably this distinguishes humans from the angelic and other beings who have bodies that are not made from the physical elements of the universe.

I am not sure of the significance, but it does not say that God simply spoke and humans (and animals) suddenly appeared as full-grown mature adults. It does say that animals and humans were built with materials that God had already created. Apparently, there was a process involved. Is it possible to call that process some form of a divinely guided evolution? Is it possible that Adam's body was born from a subhuman or proto human species (that is now extinct) and that God breathed into him the breath of life to make him human? If God made a superhuman God-man named Jesus to be born from a human virgin mother named Mary, couldn't He have made a human named Adam to be born from a subhuman mother? When the Bible refers to Jesus as the second Adam, is it telling us that the first Adam was also divinely conceived from a virgin mother of a lower species? I don't know. However, I do know that when I arrive in the New Jerusalem and walk through the pearly gates onto the streets of gold, if they tell me that Adam had a mother who was a highly developed but subhuman being, I don't think I am going to say, "Excuse me, but I must be in the wrong city."

So, what is the *breath of life* that God breathed into Adam? Is it simply the difference between inanimate and animate? Is it the thing that made a clay statue stand up, walk around, breath, see, feel, and think? Is the breath of life the thing that we today recognize as life or is it some higher spirit? The breath of life seems to be the thing that separates us from all the rest of the physical created beings. It makes us special. The breath of life that God breathed into Adam seems to be the thing that gives us the capacity for abstract thinking and the capacity to communicate with a creator God.

It may also be the thing that gives us a spirit that exists outside of the physical host body that God designed for us. There is a growing body of evidence from things like interviews with people who have had near-death experiences that indicates that some part of our being continues to exist after our host body has died. As Christians, we believe we have an eternal soul or spirit. We take it by faith. However, the concept is also being supported by these evidences. Interviews with people who have had unique experiences may not be, technically speaking, scientific data, because we cannot design an experiment to support the conclusions from the observations. Nonetheless, they are evidence.

Science has struggled to identify the element of human beings that makes us truly unique and different from the animals. Some choose to believe that humans are simply another animal, the latest and most advanced in a long line of evolved species. They believe our primary uniqueness is our larger brains. However, the difference between humans and animals is much more than the ability to walk upright, use opposable thumbs, and make tools. No other species can think, evaluate, and conclude quite the way we can. Humans are so much higher functioning than any animal that it is hard to imagine there was a simple twist of random mutation that produced a human from a subhuman. In fact, the difference between humans and animals is so great that some think humans came here from another planet—somewhere that has a more highly developed civilization.

Humans are truly unique in one very critical factor. Every civilization since the start of recorded history has had a belief in a god or a pantheon of gods of some sort. Humans seem to be the only animal who has a wish to communicate with a divine creator. Humans have a conscience that science has found in no other animal. No other species has ever been found to have any behavior that suggests a concept of a creator and a supreme being. No other animal is capable of worship or has a desire for worship the way humans do. We have never observed any animal doing anything that resembles worship of a creator or any god. Even the proto-human civilizations that some like to call human have not left us evidences of worshiping a creator God.

I have to believe that whatever the breath of life signifies, it is the thing that makes us human instead of simply just another animal species. Humans may have the physical body of an animal, but we have something more that animals do not have. If you simply compare physical bodies, humans may look a lot like other animals. We have a heart and a brain and a liver. We consume food and air and water. We move around. But we are much more that animals are not.

The Bible account says that man was created in the image of God. It says that about no other creature. So, what is significant about being created in the image of God? I am not 100 percent certain, but I believe the significance is that, like God, we are triune beings. As God has an intellectual component that we commonly call the Father, a physical component that we recognize as Jesus, and a spiritual component that we call the Holy Spirit, man also has three components to our being. We have a physical body, a mind (or soul or intellect), and a spirit (emotions). Like God, we are three, but we are one. We even recognize this when we say things like my body won't do what my mind wants it to. Is this image of God what the breath of life gave us? So, while I keep an open mind on the development of the human body, whether it was a mud statue or it was born from a subhuman mother, it is clear that God is the source of the human spirit and intellect.

Note that, as with God, where the Son and the Holy Spirit are subject to the will of the Father, we are also expected to have our bodies and our spirits/emotions subject to our minds. Christianity is not a religion for dummies. We are expected to fill our minds with knowledge of God and to keep our bodies and emotions under the control of our minds. Is your mind being filled with knowledge of God?

CHAPTER 13

DAY SEVEN: REST

The Bible says that on the seventh day God rested. If in fact the days of Genesis are earth focused twenty-four-hour days, then we have to ask what did God do on the eighth day? Also, if God is resting, does that mean He is asleep or totally disinterested in the course of His creation? When we think of rest today, we think of recharging our batteries because we have become tired. We need rest and sleep simply because we have the capability to become tired. If God is a God who never sleeps, obviously He needs no rest in the way that we think of it. What Moses is saying is that God stopped creating new things. His creative work was complete. So just as when our work is complete, we rest, when God's creative work was complete, He rested. Resting is simply a way to say that the creation is complete.

This is an area where science and scripture continue to disagree. Science says that the process of evolution is continuing even today. If that hypothesis is correct, we should be seeing a new species develop any day now. Humanity has been around for several thousand years, and while several new species have been discovered, there is no evidence that they have not existed for even longer than humans have existed. In fact, while we have seen zero new species formed, we have seen quite a few species become extinct, even in our recent history. Today we have a list of species that are threatened with extinction, and we try to protect them. We have no list of species that exist today that have not existed for thousands or even hundreds of thousands of years. That is because God is resting from His creative works.

I propose that on the seventh day, God is resting from His work of creation. He is not creating anything new. God is resting in the sense that He is not creating any new materials, any new forces, any new life-forms, or even any new species. It doesn't mean He is detached and disinterested, and it doesn't mean He is sleeping or dead. He is *resting* from, or He has completed, His *creative* works.

While God is resting from His creative efforts, He is very *active* in the *management* of His creation. We see Him communicating with mankind. We have even seen Him become a man in the person of Jesus. You can't get much more active than that.

So, if God rested from His creative works on the seventh day, and if He continues to rest from His creative works today, it seems reasonable to conclude that we are still in the seventh day of God's creation calendar. If we are still in the seventh day and have been in the seventh day for thousands of years, then how long is a day? I expect that today we are truly still in the seventh day, when creation has been completed and is running under the watchful eye of the Creator.

Is there another day one in the future when God will begin to create new things again? Are a new heaven and a new earth and a new Jerusalem coming on an eighth day? I don't know, but it makes for interesting speculation. What are you looking forward to?

CHAPTER 14

CONCLUSIONS

It seems that the Genesis account of creation and the observations of scientists are converging on a common timeline. From nothing, a singularity of energy appeared. Then matter appeared. Then light appeared. Then gravity appeared. Then radioactivity appeared. Then plants appeared. Then time appeared. Then egg-laying animals appeared. Then birthing animals appeared. Then humans appeared. So, if the observations of scientists have confirmed the timeline of Genesis to such a high degree, is it not realistic to conclude that a creator God inspired the writing of the Genesis account some four thousand years before any of the science was learned by men? Also, if a creator God inspired Moses to write an accurate account of creation four thousand years before the science was understood, is it not also reasonable to conclude that the rest of the Bible is also inspired by that same God?

When you try to pick apart the Genesis account of creation and analyze it, you start to find that it is not as complete an account as inquiring minds might have liked. There are a lot of questions we can ask that the account just does not answer. Does this mean the account is any less true? If I tell you that this morning I got out of bed at 6:00 a.m., took a shower, brushed my teeth, ate breakfast, went to work, came home, ate dinner, and went to bed at 10:00 p.m., is my account any less true because I did not tell you what I did at work or what I ate at every meal? If later I tell you that I ate a meal at noon, can you say that this is an inconsistency in my story because my earlier account said I was at work all day?

In chapter 1 of Genesis, we read an account of creation, and in chapter 2, we read another account that adds details. There seems to be some disagreement between the two accounts. For example, chapter 1 says that plants were created first, before man, but chapter 2 seems to say that man was created before any shrub of the field had appeared on the earth. Critics grab onto these apparent contradictions to say that the Bible is an unreliable book filled with errors, so it must not be true. However, is it not possible that the two accounts are both true and that we simply do not have enough information in a few hundred words to allow us to know every detail about everything that happened in the exact sequence that it happened?

The bottom line here is that, regardless of the exact sequence of each detail, the exact elapsed time, or the exact process, the design and the energy for a universe of incredible complexity made from seventeen subatomic particles and four basic forces plus the design and energy behind the first material beings with life came from the one and only omnipotent, omniscient, eternal being that we call God. The exact process and detailed timeline God used may not be fully understood, but there was nothing random or accidental about it.

In the past one hundred years—just a couple of generations—the knowledge collectively held by mankind has exploded. With each new discovery, we climb a rung higher on the ladder of understanding our universe and its origins. However, no matter how high we climb that ladder, we are always going to find God at the top.

By the way, a confirmed account of creation is not the only evidence for a creator God who is active in the management of His creation. The God who created time inspired men to write detailed prophecies of future events that have been fulfilled in exacting detail. These also confirm the divine inspiration of the Bible, but that is the subject of other books.

So why have I spent so much focus on the subject of creation? If you choose to believe the traditional six-day interpretation of Genesis, and you choose to believe all of the observations of the scientific community are incorrect and invalid, and if your faith is solid and unwavering in that concept, then I am quite happy for you. However, if you accept that some of the observations of the scientific community are true and valid, and if that challenges your faith, then I want you to know there is an alternate interpretation of Genesis that can be totally valid and consistent with much of what science has discovered about God's creation. So, whether you choose to believe God created everything in a mature state over a period of six rotations of planet earth about six thousand years ago, or whether, as I propose, you choose to believe God created everything in six creative episodes each with a duration suitable to a timeless eternal creator, it is vitally important for you to be fully convinced that there is a God, that we have been created by that God, and that He alone is worthy of our ultimate respect and obedience. Also, since there is a creator God, it stands to reason that He and He alone has the moral and legal authority to set the rules under which His creation, and we His created creatures, must operate. God has the moral and legal right to manage His creation in the way that pleases Him. The fact that we sometimes do not understand His reasons or purposes, and the fact that sometimes we may not like or agree with His rules, does not make Him any less the ultimate authority.

In a very practical application, if you are going to get the most out of your life, does it not make sense to live that life in harmony with the operating instructions given by the Creator of that life? Psychologists tell us that the happiest and most satisfied people are Christians who are living their faith. I guess it stands to reason that if you follow the instructions of the designer and maker, you get better results.

In your life, you are going to serve the will of someone with higher authority and greater power than your own. You need to accept that the highest authority in your life must be God almighty. Many who do not want to accept God as their highest authority will do everything possible to convince themselves and you that there is no creator. Most of us have grown up in an environment that has for many years scoffed at the concept of a creator God. The scoffers will ridicule you and call you an ignorant flat-earther and worse. However, the plain truth is that the deeper scientists look into the past and the origins of the universe, the more they are confirming the account in Genesis. You need to be sure in your own mind that the account of creation holds up to scientific scrutiny so you can have no doubts regarding who made you and whom you need to serve. You also need to be convinced that the Bible is the inspired Word from that creator God, so you can study His will with confidence.

The conclusion is this. There is a God. He did create you. What are you going to do about it? Will you accept His way, obey Him, and serve Him, or will you reject His way and try to live life your own way? Chose you this day whom you will serve … but as for me and my house, we will serve the Lord.

The following scriptures from the KJV and NIV of the Bible have been referenced in this book:

Gen. 1:1 (KJV)—In the beginning God created the heavens and the earth.

Gen. 1:1 (NIV)—In the beginning God created the heavens and the earth.

Gen. 1:5b (KJV)—And the evening and the morning were the first day.

Gen. 1:5b (NIV)—And there was evening and there was morning—the first day.

Gen. 1:8b (KJV)—And the evening and the morning were the second day.

Gen. 1:8b (NIV)—And there was evening and there was morning—the second day.

Gen. 1:13 (KJV)—And the evening and the morning were the third day.

Gen. 1:13 (NIV)—And there was evening and there was morning—the third day.

Gen. 1:19 (KJV)—And the evening and the morning were the fourth day

Gen. 1:19 (NIV)—And there was evening and there was morning—the fourth day.

Gen. 1:23 (KJV)—And the evening and the morning were the fifth day.

Gen. 1:23 (NIV)— And there was evening and there was morning—the fifth day.

Gen. 1:31b (KJV)—And the evening and the morning were the sixth day.

Gen. 1:31b (NIV)—And there was evening and there was morning—the sixth day.

Gen. 1:2a (KJV)—And the earth was without form, and void; and darkness was upon the face of the deep.

Gen. 1:2a (NIV)—Now the earth was formless and empty, and darkness was over the face of the deep.

Gen. 1:3 (KJV)—And God said Let there be light: and there was light.

Gen. 1:3 (NIV)—And God said, "Let there be light," and there was light

Gen. 1:6–7 (KJV)—And God said Let there be a firmament in the midst of the waters and let it divide the waters from the waters. And God made the firmament, and divided the waters which were under the firmament from the waters which were above the firmament: and it was so.

Gen. 1:6–7 (NIV)—And God said," Let there be an expanse between the waters to separate water from water." So God made the expanse and separated the water under the expanse from the water above it.

Gen. 1:9 (KJV)—And God said, Let the waters under the heaven be gathered together unto one place, and let the dry land appear; and it was so.

Gen. 1:9 (NIV)—And God said, "Let the water under the sky be gathered to one place, and let dry ground appear". And it was so.

Gen. 1:11 (KJV)—And God said, let the earth bring forth grass, the herb yielding seed, and the fruit tree yielding fruit after his kind, whose seed is in itself, upon the earth: and it was so.

Gen. 1:11 (NIV)—Then God said, "Let the land produce vegetation: seed-bearing plants and trees on the land that bear fruit with seed in it according to their various kinds." And it was so.

Gen. 1:14 (KJV)—And God said Let there be lights in the firmament of the heaven to divide the day from the night; and let them be for signs and for seasons, for days and for years.

Gen. 1:14 (NIV)—And God said, "Let there be lights in the expanse of the sky to separate the day from the night, and let them serve as signs to mark seasons and days and years.

Gen. 1:16a (KJV)—And God made two great lights; the greater light to rule the day, and the lesser light to rule the night.

Gen. 1:16a (NIV)—God made two great lights—the greater light to govern the day and the lesser light to govern the night.

Gen. 1:20 (KJV)—And God said, let the waters bring forth abundantly the moving creature that hath life, and fowl that may fly above the earth in the open firmament of heaven.

Gen. 1:20 (NIV)—And God said, "Let the water team with living creatures, and let birds fly across the expanse of the sky."

Gen. 1:22 (KJV)—And God blessed them, saying be fruitful, and multiply, and fill the waters in the seas, and let fowl multiply in the earth.

Gen. 1:22 (NIV)—God blessed them and said, "Be fruitful and increase n number and fill the waters of the seas, and let the birds increase on the earth."

Gen. 1:24 (KJV)—And God said, Let the earth bring forth the living creature after his kind, cattle and creeping thing, and beast of the earth after his kind; and it was so.

Gen. 1:24 (NIV)—And God said, "Let the land produce living creatures according to their kinds: livestock, creatures that move along the ground, and wild animals." And it was so.

Gen. 1:26a (KJV)—And God said Let us make man in our image, after our likeness …

Gen. 1:26a (NIV)—Then God said, "Let us make man in our image, in our likeness …

Gen. 1:10b (KJV)—And God saw that it was good

Gen. 1:10b (NIV)—And God saw that it was good.

Gen. 1:12b (KJV)—And God saw that it was good

Gen. 1:12b (NIV)—And God saw that it was good.

Gen. 1:18b (KJV)—And God saw that it was good

Gen. 1:18b (NIV)—And God saw that it was good.

Gen. 1:21b (KJV)—And God saw that it was good

Gen. 1:21b (NIV)—And God saw that it was good.

Gen. 1:25b (KJV)—And God saw that it was good

Gen. 1:25b (NIV)—And God saw that it was good.

Gen. 1:31a (KJV)—And God saw everything that he had made, and behold, it was very good.

Gen. 1:31a (NIV)—And God saw all that he had made, and it was very good.

Gen. 2:1 (KJV)—And the heavens and the earth were finished, and all the host of them.

Gen. 2:1 (NIV)—Thus the heavens and the earth were completed in all their vast array.

Gen. 2:2a (KJV)—And on the seventh day God ended his work which he had made; and he rested on the seventh day from all his work which he had made.

Gen. 2:2a (NIV)—By the seventh day God had finished the work he had been doing: so on the seventh day he rested from all his work.

Gen. 2:5–7 (KJV)—And every plant of the field before it was in the earth, and every herb of the field before it grew ... And the Lord God formed man of the dust of the ground ...

Gen. 2:5–7 (NIV)—When the Lord God made the earth and the heavens—and no shrub of the field had yet appeared on the earth ... the Lord God formed the man from the dust of the ground ...

Gen. 2:7 (KJV)—And the Lord God formed man of the dust of the ground, and breathed into his nostrils the breath of life; and man became a living soul.

Gen. 2:7 (NIV)—The Lord God formed the man from the dust of the ground and breathed into his nostrils the breath of life, and the man became a living being.

Gen. 2:8 (KJV)—And the Lord God planted a garden eastward in Eden; and there he put the man he had formed.

Gen. 2:8 (NIV)—Now the Lord God had planted a garden in the east in Eden; and there he put the man he had formed.

Gen. 6:1–2 (KJV)—And it came to pass, when men began to multiply on the face of the earth, and daughters were born to them, that the sons of God saw the daughters of men that they were fair; and they took them wives of all which they chose

Gen. 6:1-2 (NIV)—When men began to increase in number on the earth and daughters were born to them, the sons of God saw that the daughters of men were beautiful, and they married any of them they chose.

Joshua 24:15 (KJV) – chose you this day whom you will serve …. But as for me and my house, we will serve the Lord

Joshua 24:15 (NIV) – chose for yourselves this day whom you will serve …. But as for me and my household, we will serve the Lord.

John 2:9a (KJV)—When the ruler of the feast had tasted the water that was made wine.

John 2:9a (NIV)—And the master of the banquet tasted the water that had been turned into wine.

John 14:2a (KJV)—In my father's house are many mansions.

John 14:2a (NIV)—In my father's house are many rooms.

Heb. 11:3 (KJV)—Through faith we understand that the worlds were framed by the word of God, so that things which are seen were not made of things which do appear.

Heb. 11:3 (NIV)—By faith we understand that the universe was formed at God's command, so that what is seen was not made out of what was visible.

2 Peter 3:8 (KJV)—But beloved, be not ignorant of this one thing, that one day is with the Lord as a thousand years, and a thousand years as one day.

2 Peter 3:8 (NIV)—But do not forget this one thing, dear friends: With the Lord a day is like a thousand years, and a thousand years are like a day.

Rev 21:23 (KJV) – And the city had no need of the sun

Rev 21:23 (NIV) – The city does not need the sun

Rev 22:2 (KJV) – on either side of the river, was there the tree of life, which bare twelve manner of fruits, and yielded her fruit every month

Rev 22:2 (NIV) – On each side of the river stood the tree of life, bearing twelve crops of fruit, yielding its fruit every month.

Ken Goss was born in Savanna, Illinois, to parents of modest means who loved the Lord and their family. He attended public high school in Mt. Carroll, Illinois, and then earned an engineering degree from LeTourneau College in Longview, Texas, and an MBA from the University of Detroit.

Ken grew up in an independent, fundamental church and accepted Jesus Christ as his Lord and King at age eight. Having trusted Christ to save him from a life of sin and an eternity of torment, Ken became a lifelong student of the Bible and an active church member.

Ken has spent more than forty years as an engineer in the auto industry, traveling between Michigan, Brazil, Italy, and Germany. He has been married for forty-eight years to his high school sweetheart, and together they cherish four children and nine grandchildren.

Ken makes his home in Clarkston, Michigan.

Printed in the United States
By Bookmasters